D1636101

Baseball TRIVIA QUIZ BOOK

·TRIVIAL TRUTHS·

BARNES &NOBLE BOOKS
B O O K S
NEW YORK

The author wishes to thank all those who provided questions, expertise, and encouragement: Carol Kelly–Gangi, Frank Hoffman, Stuart Miller, Sharon Bosley, Rick Campbell, Sui Mon Wu, John Gangi, Howard Kelly, Tom Kelly, Steve Lysaker, Stephen Lynn, Hunter Hauk, Tommy Jenkins, Don Stefanelli, and Bill Rankin.

2000 Barnes & Noble Books

ISBN 0-7607-2104-1

Text design by Lundquist Design, New York

Printed and bound in the United States of America

01 02 03 MP 9 8 7 6 5 4 3

OPM

Q: What pitcher won the very first Cy Young Award?

Q: Who was Cy Young?

Q: Name the oldest player to appear in a major-league game.

Q: Who was the first player to play all nine positions in one game?

Q: What father-and-son teammates hit back-to-back homers in the same inning?

A: The Cy Young Award was given for the first time in 1956; Don Newcombe won the now-coveted award pitching for the Brooklyn Dodgers. The first year that the award was given to a player in each league was 1967.

A: Denton True "Cy" Young, baseball's winningest pitcher, was a right-hander who won 511 games during his career in the majors, which began in 1890. He was nicknamed "Cyclone," later shortened to "Cy," because he once splintered a fence with one of his fastballs.

A: Satchel Paige. He threw three shutout innings for the Kansas City Athletics against the Boston Red Sox at the age of fifty-nine—if not older—on September 25, 1965.

A: Bert Campaneris performed this amazing feat for the Kansas City A's on September 8, 1965.

A: Ken Griffey Sr. and Ken Griffey Jr., for the Seattle Mariners on September 14, 1990. California's Kirk McCaskill was the pitcher.

Q: Name the only major-league pitcher to throw back-to-back no-hitters?

Q: Name the existing teams, eight from the American League and eight from the National League, and the cities where they played as of 1902.

Q: What pitcher is the all-time leader for relief wins in a single season?

Q: What pitcher has the record for most saves in a single season?

A: Johnny Vander Meer, pitching for the Cincinnati Reds in 1938. After the historic performance against the Braves and the Dodgers, his nicknames became "Double No Hit" and "The Dutch Master."

A: *American League:*
NY Yankees
Boston Red Sox
Detroit Tigers
Washington Senators
St. Louis Browns
Chicago White Sox
Philadelphia Athletics
Cleveland Indians

National League:
St. Louis Cardinals
Philadelphia Phillies
Boston Braves
NY Giants
Chicago Cubs
Cincinnati Reds
Pittsburgh Pirates
Brooklyn Dodgers

A: Elroy Face of the Pittsburgh Pirates had eighteen relief wins in 1959.

A: Bobby Thigpen of the Chicago White Sox had fifty-seven saves in 1990.

Q: What father and son pitchers hold the record for combined career wins in the majors?

Q: Who hit "the shot heard around the world"?

Q: What famous slugger, who also donned a New York uniform, was born on that very day?

Q: Who is the all-time leader for triples in a season?

Q: What Hall of Fame pitcher, who was named after a U.S. President, was played in a movie by a future President?

A: Mel and Todd Stottlemyre (over 300 wins and counting).

A: Bobby Thomson of the New York Giants hit this homer—infamous to all Brooklyn Dodger fans—off Ralph Branca to lead his team to the World Series on October 3, 1951. The Giants won the game 5–4, and the pennant.

A: Dave Winfield, who played for the Yankees during the 1980s.

A: Pittsburgh's Chief Wilson had thirty-six triples in 1912.

A: Grover Cleveland Alexander of the Philadelphia Phillies, Chicago Cubs, and St. Louis Cardinals, was played by then-actor Ronald Reagan in the 1952 film *The Winning Team*.

Q: What pitcher in baseball's modern era holds the record for the lowest single season ERA?

Q: How many batting titles did Boston's Ted Williams win? Give the years and batting averages for extra credit.

Q: How many MVP awards did Yogi Berra win and in what years?

Q: What team holds the distinction of losing twenty-three straight games?

Q: Who were the only brothers to have combined for more than forty wins in a single season as team-mates?

A: Bob Gibson of the St. Louis Cardinals, with an ERA of 1.12 in 1968.

A: Six.

Year	Average
1941	.406
1942	.356
1947	.343
1948	.369
1957	.388
1958	.328

A: Three. 1951, 1954, and 1955.

A: The Philadelphia Phillies of 1961.

A: Dizzy Dean (30) and his brother Paul (19) did it for the 1934 St. Louis Cardinals.

Q: Who holds the major league record for career grand slams?

Q: Name the four New York Yankee Cy Young Award winners. Give the years they won for extra credit.

Q: Who is the only hitter in baseball history to win a batting title in three separate decades?

Q: What pitcher holds the major-league record for most lifetime shutouts?

Q: Six batsmen have hit .300 or better for at least fifteen consecutive years. Can you name them?

A: Lou Gehrig of the New York Yankees with a grand total of twenty-three.

A: Bob Turley (1958)
Whitey Ford (1961)
Sparky Lyle (1977)
Ron Guidry (1978)

A: The Kansas City Royals George Brett, in 1976, 1980, and 1990. Surprisingly, Ty Cobb's batting titles were all between 1907 and 1919, none in the 1920s.

A: Washington Senator Walter Johnson, with 110.

A: Ty Cobb, Cap Anson, Honus Wagner, Stan Musial, Ted Williams, and Rod Carew.

Q: Who was the last pitcher to win thirty or more games in a season?

Q: What major-league hurler co-starred with Elliot Gould in Robert Altman's 1973 film *The Long Goodbye*?

Q: In the 1950s, a decade dominated by New York teams, what was the only year that a New York team failed to make it to the World Series?

Q: Who struck out seventeen Detroit Tigers in one game of the 1968 World Series?

Q: Who was the first Hispanic player elected to the Hall of Fame?

A: Denny McLain had thirty-one wins for the Detroit Tigers in 1968. He ended up leading them to the American League pennant and the world championship.

A: Jim Bouton.

A: 1959. The Los Angeles Dodgers (who before 1958 played in Brooklyn) and the Chicago White Sox faced off that year.

A: Bob Gibson, playing for the St. Louis Cardinals.

A: Pittsburgh Pirate Roberto Clemente, Puerto Rican by birth and one of the true heroes of American baseball, was inducted in 1973.

Q: What player holds the all-time major-league hit record? What's the magic number?

Q: What player can boast the most Gold Glove Awards?

Q: Who is the major-league pitcher with an uncanny 363 lifetime wins and 363 career hits?

Q: Name the one major leaguer to win MVP Awards in both leagues.

A: Pete Rose with 4,256 hits.

A: Third-baseman Brooks Robinson and pitcher Jim Kaat are tied with sixteen a piece.

A: Warren Spahn, who pitched for the Boston (later Milwaukee) Braves, as well as the New York Mets and the San Francisco Giants.

A: Frank Robinson. He won with Cincinnati (NL) in 1961 and Baltimore (AL) in 1966.

Q: True or False: Ted Williams never got 200 hits in a season.

Q: What two pitchers in the 1984 All-Star Game combined to strike out six American League players consecutively?

Q: What National League team finished last in the standings the same year they had a .315 team batting average?

Q: What year was the first World Series played? Give the outcome for extra credit.

Q: What area of Detroit's Tiger Stadium (then called Navin Field) was known as "Cobb's Lake"?

A: True. The closest he came was 194 in 1949.

A: Dwight Gooden and Fernando Valenzuela.

A: The 1930 Philadelphia Phillies.

A: 1903. The Boston Pilgrims defeated the Pittsburgh Pirates five games to three.

A: It was an area in front of home plate that was watered down by the grounds crew to help Ty Cobb lay down perfect bunts.

Q: What skipper had the longest career as a manager in the majors?

Q: Cursed or not—what year did the Boston Red Sox win their last World Series?

Q: What is the "curse of the Bambino"?

Q: For extra credit, how much money did Boston get for the "curse of the Bambino"?

Q: In 1994 (which was a strike-shortened season), Chuck Knoblauch hit forty-five doubles for the Minnesota Twins. Who holds the all-time record for doubles in a single season?

A: Connie Mack, with a managing career that spanned fifty years. He also holds the record for the most wins (3,582) and the most losses (3,814).

A: 1918.

A: It refers to the Boston Red Sox team's inability to win a World Series after Babe Ruth was sold (not even traded!) to the Yankees in 1920.

A: The curse continues when attempting to verify the exact amount for which Sox owner Harry Frazee sold Ruth. Estimates range from $25,000 to $125,000 with a $300,000 loan.

A: Earl Webb. He hit sixty-seven doubles for the Boston Red Sox in 1931.

Q: Who were the first African-American managers in the American and National Leagues?

Q: Who was the first African-American player to break the color barrier in the American League?

Q: In Mickey Mantle's 1956 MVP, Triple Crown year, how many home runs and RBIs did he have? Give his batting average for extra credit.

Q: What year did Roger Maris hit sixty-one home runs?

Q: How many no-hitters did Nolan Ryan pitch?

A: One man was the first in both leagues. Frank Robinson became an American League manager with Cleveland in 1975 and a National League manager with San Francisco in 1981.

A: Larry Doby, playing for the Cleveland Indians in 1947. He did this three months after Jackie Robinson became the first African American in the major leagues.

A: Fifty-two home runs, 130 RBIs, and .353 batting average.

A: 1961, with the New York Yankees. That same year, Mantle hit fifty-four.

A: Seven—his career record has yet to be broken. Sandy Koufax is next in line with four.

Q: The St. Louis Browns played their last game in 1953. What team did they become?

Q: In 1964, the Yankees played the last World Series in their so-called Dynasty Years. Who beat them?

Q: Name the top five players in number of batting titles won.

Q: When was the first World Series MVP awarded? Who won it?

Q: How many times did the Brooklyn Dodgers win the World Series?

A: The Baltimore Orioles.

A: The St. Louis Cardinals. The Bronx Bombers didn't win the Series again until 1977.

A: Ty Cobb (12)
Honus Wagner (8)
Tony Gwynn (8)
Rod Carew (7)
Stan Musial (7)

A: Johnny Podres pitched his way to the award for the Brooklyn Dodgers in 1955.

A: Once, in 1955. They met more success in Los Angeles.

Q: What year was the first All-Star Game played?
   a. 1936
   b. 1933
   c. 1927
   d. 1906

Q: True or False: The All-Star Game was initially planned as a tie-in to the Chicago World's Fair.

Q: Who was the last Triple Crown winner?

Q: Only one World Series game has been cancelled due to an earthquake. When and where was it cancelled?

Q: Who holds the American League record for most lifetime home runs by a right-handed batter?

A: b.

A: True. It's been an annual event—save for 1945—ever since. There were actually two games played each year from 1959 to 1962.

A: Boston Red Sox player Carl Yastrzemski in 1967 with 44 home runs, 121 RBIs, and a .326 batting average.

A: On October 17, 1989, an earthquake before Game Three delayed the "World Series by the Bay" between the San Francisco Giants and the Oakland Athletics. Sixty-seven people in the Bay Area were killed, and the series was delayed ten days. The Athletics ended up sweeping the series in four games.

A: Harmon Killebrew, who played for the Senators and the Twins, with 573.

Q: What batter has the record for the highest lifetime batting average?

Q: Who holds the record for most grand slam home runs in a single season?

Q: What pitcher holds the record for the most career innings pitched?

Q: Who holds the record for total bases in a single season?

Q: Who is the all-time leader in number of games saved?

A: Ty Cobb, who batted .367.

A: Don Mattingly, of the New York Yankees, had six in 1987.

A: Cy Young, with 7,356 innings pitched.

A: Babe Ruth had 457 total bases in 1921.

A: Lee Smith, with 478 saves, pitched most of his career for the Cubs, Red Sox, and Cardinals, and also played for the Orioles, Yankees, Angels, Reds, and Expos.

Q: What year did Joe DiMaggio hit in fifty-six straight games? Give the number of times Joltin' Joe struck out that whole year for extra credit.

Q: Who is the only player to hit two grand slams in the same inning?

Q: Here are the nicknames. Can you fill in these players' real names?

The Big Train   _____

The Human Vacuum Cleaner   _____

The Penguin   _____

The Big Unit   _____

The Grand Old Man   _____

The Barber   _____

The Iron Horse   _____

Louisiana Lightnin'   _____

The Yankee Clipper   _____

Baseball's Quiet Man   _____

The Flying Dutchman   _____

A: 1941. He struck out a meager thirteen times.

A: Though he'd never hit one before, Fernando Tatis hit two grand slams in the same inning for the St. Louis Cardinals on April 23, 1999.

A: Walter Johnson
     Brooks Robinson
     Ron Cey
     Randy Johnson
     Connie Mack
     Sal Maglie
     Lou Gehrig
     Ron Guidry
     Joe DiMaggio
     Bill Dickey
     Honus Wagner

Q: Name the top three major-league career home run leaders as of the beginning of the 2000 season.

Q: Which major-league baseball stadium was the last to install lights?

Q: When was the first night baseball game played?

Q: How many times did St. Louis Cardinal Stan Musial win the National League MVP Award?

Q: What are the three oldest ballparks?

A: Hank Aaron   755
   Babe Ruth   714
   Willie Mays 660

A: Chicago's Wrigley Field. The Cubs played their first night game on August 6, 1988.

A: The Reds and the Phillies played the first night game on May 24, 1935, at Crosley Field in Cincinnati. The Reds beat the Phillies 2–1 after President Franklin Delano Roosevelt activated the lights by pressing a button in the White House.

A: He won three times, in 1943, 1946, and 1948.

A: Fenway Park (1912), with a capacity of 33,871; Wrigley Field (1914), which holds 38,884, and Yankee Stadium (1923), which was renovated in 1974-75 and holds 57,545.

Q: What Yankee slugger averaged 143 RBIs a year over eleven years?

Q: Who was the only Yankee to win both the Rookie of the Year Award and the MVP Award?

Q: Name the only pitcher to hurl a no-hitter on opening day.

Q: True or False: The most recent unassisted triple play was made by Boston's John Valentin on July 8, 1994.

Q: What 1910 double-play combination was made famous by a poem published in the *New York World*?

A: Lou Gehrig.

A: Thurman Munson (Rookie of the Year Award 1970, MVP 1976).

A: Cleveland Indian Bob Feller did it in 1940 against the Chicago White Sox. The final score was 1–0.

A: False. Randy Velarde of Oakland made one while playing against the Yankees in New York on Memorial Day, 2000—becoming the first player in major-league history to do so in any New York stadium.

A: Chicago Cubs Joe Tinker, Johnny Evers, and Frank Chance inspired the terminology "Tinker to Evers to Chance," which has been used ever since to describe a smooth double play. A poem, "Baseball's Sad Lexicon," written by Franklin P. Adams, immortalized this famous combination.

Q: Only one member of the original 1962 New York Mets is still in uniform today. Who is he, and where is he suited up?

Q: For extra credit, what are this player's two nicknames?

Q: In 1972, the Philadelphia Phillies had a dismal record of 59–97. What was a bright spot for the team that year?

Q: What pitcher hit an inside-the-park grand slam in 1965, becoming the first hurler to do so since 1910?

Q: Who is the most recent twenty-five game loser?

A: Don Zimmer, who played third base for the Mets in 1962. These days he dons a uniform for the Yankees as their bench coach.

A: Don Zimmer is nicknamed "Zim" and "Popeye."

A: Pitcher Steve Carlton won the Cy Young Award and the Triple Crown for pitchers with a record of 27–10, an ERA of 1.97, and 310 strikeouts. Responsible for nearly half of the team's wins that season, Carlton holds the record for the most wins by a pitcher on a team with a losing record.

A: Mel Stottlemyre did it for the 1965 New York Yankees.

A: Ben Cantwell, with a record of 4–25 for the Boston Braves in 1935.

Q: What player was known for greeting reporters with the words, "What a great day for baseball. Let's play two!"?

Q: What player holds the record for the most RBIs in a single season?

Q: What player had the fewest RBIs in a single season with a minimum of five hundred at bats?

Q: Name the only three switch-hitters in major-league history to get forty or more home runs in a single season?

Q: What future Hall of Famer won twenty-seven games in his final season?

A: Ernie "Mr. Cub" Banks, who played for Chicago from 1953 to 1973. He led the league in RBIs (143) in 1959 and homers in 1960, with forty-one. He was named MVP two years in a row (1958-59), even though his team was tied for fifth place out of eight teams.

A: Hack Wilson, who knocked in 190 runs for the Chicago Cubs in 1930.

A: Enzo Hernandez of the San Diego Padres holds the record with twelve RBIs in 549 at bats in 1971.

A: Mickey Mantle, New York Yankees
Todd Hundley, New York Mets
Ken Caminiti, San Diego Padres

A: Sandy Koufax for the LA Dodgers in 1966.

Q: Hall of Fame inductees are most likely to have played what position?

Q: What position accounts for the least number of Hall of Famers?

Q: Why was the Hall of Fame put in Cooperstown, New York?

Q: What player inspired a ruling that "any player on (major-league) baseball's ineligible list shall not be an eligible candidate" for the Hall of Fame?

Q: Why is Shoeless Joe Jackson not in the Hall of Fame?

A: Pitcher. Fifty-eight Hall of Famers have been inducted as pitchers.

A: Third base. Only nine third basemen have made it to Cooperstown.

A: Because Cooperstown is believed to be the place where Abner Doubleday devised the first scheme for playing baseball in 1839.

A: Pete Rose, because of illegal gambling activities that had made him ineligible to participate in Organized Baseball.

A: Joe Jackson was placed on baseball's ineligible list as a result of his involvement in "fixing" the 1919 World Series.

Q: What Harvard graduate, who played for the Indians, Phillies, Reds, and Giants, was also the only major-leaguer killed in action during World War I?

Q: What Hall of Fame pitcher for the New York Giants died from tuberculosis he had contracted as a result of exposure to poisonous gas during World War I?

Q: What Hall of Famer died at the age of forty-nine after being struck by a drunk driver in New Orleans?

Q: What former major-league player died in 1958 when the NJ Central Lines train on which he was riding plunged from an open drawbridge into Newark Bay?

A: Eddie Grant, who retired in 1916 with a lifetime batting average of .249. In 1918, he was killed in action in France at the age of thirty-five.

A: Christy Mathewson died in 1925; he began his career in 1901, winning twenty games for the New York Giants.

A: Mel Ott, a New York Giants slugger who was known for raising his right leg before swinging. He had 511 career home runs.

A: George "Snuffy" Stirnweiss, second baseman for the Yankees in the 1940s.

Q: Can you name the team that plays (or played) in each of these fields?

> Forbes Field
> Crosley Field
> Briggs Stadium
> Municipal Stadium
> Metrodome
> Skydome
> Wrigley Field
> Veterans Stadium
> Comiskey Park
> Camden Yards

Q: Who was the last player to make more than forty errors in a season?

Q: What team was referred to as the Yankees of the Negro Leagues?

A: Pittsburgh Pirates
    Cincinnati Reds
    Detroit Tigers
    Cleveland Indians
    Minnesota Twins
    Toronto Blue Jays
    Chicago Cubs
    Philadelphia Phillies
    Chicago White Sox
    Baltimore Orioles

A: Shortstop Jose Offerman made forty-two errors for Los Angeles in 1992, the most by a Dodgers shortstop in fifty-one years.

A: The Kansas City Monarchs, who won more than a dozen championships in their thirty-seven seasons.

Q: Who is the only hitter to crush more than fifty life-time homers at both Yankee Stadium and Fenway Park?

Q: Name the Hall of Famer who hit into four triple plays in his career.

Q: What Red Sox great and future Hall of Famer was also a fighter pilot in World War II and Korea?

Q: What player holds the record for the most consecutive years with thirty or more home runs (twelve years, to be exact)?

A: Mike Stanley started with the Yanks in 1992, and has since played for both Boston and New York.

A: Brooks Robinson of the Orioles.

A: Ted Williams, who, despite missing the better part of five seasons, had a .344 lifetime batting average and 521 career home runs.

A: Jimmie Foxx, every year from 1929 to 1940. For the first seven years of the streak, Foxx played for the Philadelphia A's, and in 1939 he went to the Boston Red Sox.

Q: What two major-league catchers grew up as friends in the same neighborhood of St. Louis?

Q: Who was the only major-league player to play 500 games each as a catcher, first baseman, and third baseman?

Q: What batter holds the record for the most walks in a single season?

Q: Who is the career leader in RBIs?

Q: What pitcher has the lowest career ERA?

A: Hall of Fame catcher Yogi Berra of the Yankees and Joe Garagiola, better known as an announcer, who caught for the Cardinals and the Pirates.

A: Joe Torre, who played for the Braves, Cardinals, and Mets.

A: Babe Ruth had 170 walks in 1923.

A: Hank Aaron, with 2,297.

A: "Big Ed" Walsh, who had a 1.82 ERA over fourteen seasons from 1904 to 1917, most of them with the Chicago White Sox.

Q: What major-league pitcher holds the modern record for most wins in a single season?

Q: Who was the Yankees' owner in 1920, when they acquired Babe Ruth from the Red Sox?

Q: Who holds the record for most career home runs by a catcher?

Q: Who holds the modern major-league record for having the highest single season batting average?

Q: What team was called the "Gashouse Gang"? Where did they get their name?

A: Jack Chesbro had forty-one wins in 1904 playing for the New York Yankees.

A: Colonel Jacob Ruppert, who owned the team from 1915 to 1939.

A: Carlton Fisk, of both the Red Sox and the White Sox, with 376 homers. Johnny Bench had 389 career homers, but he was not a catcher during every season of his career.

A: Rogers Hornsby of the St. Louis Cardinals, with a .424 average in 1924. He was considered the game's greatest right-handed hitter, taking home seven batting championships and two MVP Awards.

A: The 1934 St. Louis Cardinals—including players such as Dizzy Dean, Ducky Medwick, Frankie Frisch, Leo Durocher, and Jessie Haines—got their nickname for their wackiness and hard-nose style of playing.

Q: Who was the first player to play for a team managed by his father?

Q: Since 1901, who is the oldest player to hit a grand slam home run?

Q: Who was the tallest major-league player prior to the 6'10" pitcher Randy Johnson?

Q: What pitcher holds the major-league career strike-out record?

Q: What player, in 1952, became the first rookie to homer three times in a game?

A: Earl Mack (son of Connie Mack) for the Philadelphia A's in 1910.

A: In 1991, Carlton Fisk did it at the ripe age of forty-three for the Chicago White Sox.

A: Johnny Gee. Though he only won seven games between the years of 1939 and 1946, he sets the height record at 6'9" tall. The tallest successful player in the majors before Johnson was Gene Conley—who was 6'8" and won ninety-one games for the Braves, Phillies, and Red Sox in the 1950s and 1960s. Conley was also a pro basketball player.

A: Nolan Ryan, with 5,714.

A: Eddie Mathews, for the Milwaukee Braves.

Q: What pitcher tossed a twelve-inning perfect game for the Pittsburgh Pirates, only to lose the game in the thirteenth inning?

Q: Who were the only identical twin brothers to play for the same team in the 20th century?

Q: What brother duo holds the record for career wins as pitchers?

Q: What year was the World Series cancelled due to a players' strike?

Q: What member of the U.S. Congress once pitched a perfect game in the National League?

A: Harvey Haddix on May 26, 1959. The Pirates lost the game to the Braves by a score of 1–0.

A: Johnny and Eddie O'Brien, who played for the Pittsburgh Pirates from 1953 through 1958.

A: Joe and Phil Niekro, with a combined career win total of 539.

A: 1994.

A: Jim Bunning, House Republican from Kentucky, pitched a perfect game for the Phillies in 1964.

Q: Who tied Roger Clemens's 1986 single-game strikeout record of twenty on September 18, 1996?

Q: What Hall of Famer retired on December 7, 1941—the day of the Pearl Harbor bombing—and opened a bowling alley on the same day?

Q: Denny McLain was the last American League pitcher to win over thirty games in a season. Who was the last National League pitcher to do so?

Q: What was this pitcher's full name?

A: Roger Clemens, when he beat the Tigers 4–0. Chicago Cubs Kerry Wood later tied this record in 1998.

A: Lefty Grove, who played for the Philadelphia A's from 1925 to 1933 and the Boston Red Sox from 1934 to 1941.

A: Dizzy Dean, who racked up thirty wins in 1934 for the St. Louis Cardinals.

A: Jay Hanna Dean.

Q: What Red Sox player hit twenty-four home runs and had a .530 slugging average at the age of nineteen?

Q: Speaking of teenagers, who holds the record for the most major-league wins as a teenager?

Q: Who was the youngest person to play in a major-league game?

Q: Who was the youngest player to win a batting title in the major leagues?

A: Tony Conigliaro in 1964. His twenty-four homers are the most by any teenage player in major-league history.

A: Wally Bunker—nineteen years old with nineteen wins for the Baltimore Orioles in 1964.

A: In 1944, at fifteen years of age, Joe Nuxhall pitched a game for the Cincinnati Reds.

A: Al Kaline, who hit .340 in 1955 for the Detroit Tigers. He was twenty years old.

Q: Who was the youngest player to hit a homer in a major-league game?

Q: Who was the youngest player to hit a home run in the World Series?

Q: Who was the youngest manager in the major leagues?

Q: Who was the only major-league player to win both the MVP and the Rookie of the Year Award in the same year?

A: Tommy Brown, at seventeen years old, for the 1945
    Brooklyn Dodgers.

A: Nineteen-year-old Andruw Jones did it for the Atlanta
    Braves in 1996.

A: Twenty-four-year-old Lou Boudreau, who managed the
    Cleveland Indians in 1942.

A: Fred Lynn for the Red Sox in 1975. He hit .331 that year.

Q: What pitcher holds the major-league record for most strikeouts by a rookie in a season?

Q: Though there have been several one-armed pitchers in the majors, have there ever been any one-legged pitchers?

Q: Who was the smallest man to ever play in the majors?

Q: What high-kicking, Dominican-born pitcher won twenty games or more in six seasons during the sixties?

Q: What batter has the dubious honor of holding the number one and number two spots in the record books for single-season strikeouts?

A: Dwight Gooden, who struck out 276 for the Mets in 1984 at the age of 19.

A: After losing his leg in World War II, minor-leaguer Bert Shephard was outfitted with an artificial leg and signed by the Washington Senators as a coach in 1945. On August 4th of that year, he made a relief appearance for the team—giving up only one run in five innings of play.

A: Eddie Gaedel, a midget, was 3'7" tall and weighed in at sixty-seven pounds. Gaedel was hired by Bill Veeck— owner of the Cleveland Indians and master showman—as a publicity stunt in 1951. He made an appearance in only one game.

A: San Francisco Giant Juan Marichal, the "Dominican Dandy" from Laguna Verde, was a twenty game victor in six of the seven seasons from 1963 to 1969. Although the soft-spoken, hard-throwing Marichal won more games (191) that decade than any other hurler, he never received a Cy Young Award.

A: Bobby Bonds, with 189 and 187.

Q: What is another name for a reverse curveball?

Q: What pitch requires gripping the ball with the middle and index fingers across the seams at their widest part?

Q: What pitch requires joining the index finger and thumb in a circle on the side of the ball?

Q: What Royals closer once said, "I found a delivery in my flaw"?

Q: This Cubs infielder and 1984 National League MVP had streaks of thirty or more games without an error fifteen times in his career. Name him.

A: Screwball.

A: Curveball.

A: Circle change-up.

A: Dan Quisenberry.

A: Ryne Sandberg.

Q: Though he retired with more than 250 wins, this pitcher also had more career walks than strikeouts. Who was he?

Q: Who was the last player/manager to win an MVP and a World Series?

Q: What was the name of his son-in-law, a major-league hurler who's in the record books himself?

Q: Eleven players have won back-to-back MVPs. Name them, the years they won, and the teams for which they played.

A: Ted Lyons, who played for the Chicago White Sox from 1923 to 1946.

A: Lou Boudreau for the Cleveland Indians in 1948.

A: Denny McLain.

A: 1932–33: Jimmie Foxx, Philadelphia A's
1944–45: Hal Newhouser, Detroit Tigers
1954–55: Yogi Berra, New York Yankees
1956–57: Mickey Mantle, New York Yankees
1958–59 Ernie Banks, Chicago Cubs
1960–61: Roger Maris, New York Yankees
1975–76: Joe Morgan, Cincinnati Reds
1980–81: Mike Schmidt, Philadelphia Phillies
1982–83: Dale Murphy, Atlanta Braves
1992–93: Barry Bonds, Pittsburgh Pirates,
San Francisco Giants
1993–94: Frank Thomas, Chicago White Sox

Q: The following All-Star players' numbers were well known in their day. Can you match the number to the player?

1. Mickey Mantle
2. Stan Musial
3. Ted Williams
4. Hank Aaron
5. Jackie Robinson
6. Roy Campanella
7. Willie Mays
8. Roberto Clemente

a. 9
b. 7
c. 44
d. 42
e. 39
f. 21
g. 24
h. 6

Q: True or False: A 1778 diary of a soldier at Valley Forge refers to a game of "Base" that was played among the troops.

Q: Which of the following games is generally thought of as the forerunner of American baseball?
a) Rounders
b) Cricket
c) Stool Ball
d) Bat and Ball

A: 1-b, 2-h, 3-a, 4-c, 5-d, 6-e, 7-g, 8-f

A: True.

A: a) Rounders (an English children's game), though this is
    still debated.

Q: What team is known as the first all-salaried professional club?

Q: When was the term "fan" first uttered in reference to baseball's spectators?

Q: Why is 1901 to 1919 commonly referred to as "The Dead Ball Era"?

Q: Who holds the lifetime record for lead-off homers in the major leagues?

Q: The player above also holds the record for the most stolen bases in a single season with 130. Who holds the record for the most stolen bases in a game?

A: The Cincinnati Red Stockings, who turned all-pro in 1869.

A: The term was coined by Ted Sullivan, manager of the St. Louis Browns, in 1883, referring to enthusiasts who seemed fanatical.

A: The ball that was used for play did not go as far when hit because the hand-rolled yarn was not as tight as ones in use today. In 1919, they were "juiced up" and made heavier to revive interest in the game.

A: Rickey Henderson, with seventy-eight as of the start of the 2000 season. During his long career, Henderson has played for Oakland, New York (Yankees and Mets), San Diego, Toronto, Anaheim, and Seattle.

A: Eddie Collins of the Philadelphia A's, with a grand total of six. Collins performed this feat twice: on September 11, 1912 and September 22, 1922.

Q: What two famous New York Yankee Hall of Famers also opened a bowling alley together in New Jersey?

Q: What pitcher tossed 1,727 innings without being relieved?

Q: Name the only major-league manager who also acted as a head coach in the NFL?

Q: What were the names of Joe DiMaggio's baseball-playing brothers, and what teams did they play for?

Q: From 1947 to 1953, six of the seven National League Rookies of the Year were former Negro League players. Can you name them and their teams?

A: Yogi Berra and Phil Rizzuto.

A: Jack Taylor. His unbreakable record spanned 188 games, five years, and two teams. He played for both the St. Louis Cardinals and the Chicago Cubs during this streak, which began on June 20, 1901.

A: Hugo Bezdek—he managed the Pirates from 1917 to 1919 and went on to coach the Pittsburgh Steelers.

A: Dom DiMaggio (Boston Red Sox) and Vince DiMaggio (Boston Braves, Cincinnati Reds, Pittsburgh Pirates, Philadelphia Phillies, and NY Giants).

A:
1947	Jackie Robinson	Brooklyn Dodgers
1949	Don Newcombe	Brooklyn Dodgers
1950	Sam Jethroe	Boston Braves
1951	Willie Mays	New York Giants
1952	Joe Black	Brooklyn Dodgers
1953	Jim Gilliam	Brooklyn Dodgers

Q: How many times did Roberto Clemente win the National League batting title? Give the years and batting averages for extra credit.

Q: Match the player with the college or university where he played baseball.
1. Chuck Knoblauch   a. University of Florida
2. Roger Clemens   b. San Diego State
3. Tony Gwynn   c. Yale University
4. Ron Darling   d. Texas A&M
5. Mike Stanley   e. University of Texas

Q: Who was pitcher Gaylord Perry complaining about when he made the comment, "Greaseball, greaseball, greaseball. That's all I throw him, and he still hits them."

Q: What Negro League player is credited in the Hall of Fame with hitting "almost 800 home runs"?

A: Four times:

1961	.351
1964	.339
1965	.329
1967	.357

A: 1-d, 2-e, 3-b, 4-c, 5-a

A: The Minnesota Twins Rod Carew, who hit .388 in 1977.

A: Josh Gibson, who played for Pittsburgh's Homestead Grays.

Q: Who was the last pitcher to throw a no-hitter against the New York Yankees?

Q: What two players made major-league history on April 24, 2000, when they each hit a pair of switch-hit homers in the same game?

Q: Has there ever been a player to hit for two different teams in two different cities on the same day in the history of major-league ball?

Q: New York Met pitchers have won the Cy Young Award four times. Name the pitchers and the years they won.

A: Hoyt Wilhelm of the Baltimore Orioles was the last to blank the Yanks, on September 20, 1958.

A: Yankees Jorge Posada and Bernie Williams.

A: Yes. Joel Youngblood accomplished this strange feat in 1981 when he was traded from the Mets to the Expos and played games for both teams on the same day.

A: Tom Seaver in 1969, 1973, 1975; Dwight Gooden in 1985.

Q: Who pitched the only perfect game in World Series history? How many pitches did he throw?

Q: Who was the last catcher to win a batting title?

Q: Which general manager of the Brooklyn Dodgers was responsible for bringing the first African American into the majors in 1947?

Q: Who was the first African American to play in the minor leagues?

Q: Who was the first African-American player in the major leagues?

A: Don Larsen did it for the New York Yankees on Oct. 8, 1956, with ninety-seven pitches. The Yanks won 2–0.

A: The Cincinnati Reds Ernie Lombardi batted .342 in 1938. He hit .306 for his career.

A: Branch Rickey signed Jackie Robinson, who played his first major-league game on April 15, 1947. African Americans had been barred from playing in the majors prior to this.

A: In 1878, Bud Fowler hurled three games for the Lynn Live Oaks (Lynn, Massachusetts) in the International Association, the nation's first minor league.

A: Since no African Americans played in the majors from 1899 to 1946, the technically correct answer is Moses Fleetwood Walker. He was a catcher for the Toledo Blue Stockings (who were then considered a major-league team) in 1884. Jackie Robinson became the first African-American major-league player in the modern era when he joined the Dodgers in 1947.

Q: In the 1934 All-Star Game, New York Giants pitcher Carl Hubbell struck out five consecutive American League players, among them some of the top sluggers of all time. Who were they?

Q: True or False: Ted Williams hit a triple in his last career at bat.

Q: Who was the first National League player to hit a grand slam home run in the World Series?

Q: Did Joe DiMaggio ever win a Gold Glove Award?

Q: What Negro League player stole 175 bases in one season?

A: Babe Ruth, Lou Gehrig, Jimmie Foxx, Al Simmons, and Joe Cronin—all future Hall of Famers.

A: False. He hit a homer off Oriole Jack Fisher on September 28, 1960.

A: Chuck Hiller for the San Francisco Giants in 1962.

A: No. Joltin' Joe retired in 1951, and the awards weren't given out until 1957.

A: James "Cool Papa" Bell, in 1933.

Q: Give the team names for the nicknames below:
The Whiz Kids
Dem Bums
The Ruppert Rifles

Q: Who are the only two players to have their numbers retired by the Chicago Cubs?

Q: List the four Boston Red Sox players who've had their numbers retired.

Q: What major-league manager was thrown out of ninety-one games in his career?

A: 1950 Philadelphia Phillies
Brooklyn Dodgers
New York Yankees (under the ownership of
Colonel Jacob Ruppert)

A: Ernie Banks (14) and Billy Williams (26).

A: Bobby Doerr (1), Joe Cronin (4), Carl Yastrzemski (8),
and Ted Williams (9).

A: Earl Weaver of the Baltimore Orioles.

Q: Can you match the player with the book he wrote?
1. Cal Ripken Jr.   a. *Chasing the Dream*
2. Jim Bouton   b. *My Life in Baseball*
3. Whitey Herzog   c. *Ball Four*
4. Ty Cobb   d. *You're Missing a Great Game*
5. Joe Torre   e. *The Only Way I Know*

Q: Who is the only five-time Cy Young Award winner?

Q: What president started the tradition of throwing out the first ball on opening day?

Q: Name the president who did it the most times.

Q: Finally, name the first Commander-in-Chief to break this time-honored practice.

A: 1-e, 2-c, 3-d, 4-b, 5-a

A: Roger Clemens, in 1986, 1987, 1991, 1997, and 1998.

A: William Howard Taft in 1910.

A: Franklin D. Roosevelt (8).

A: Jimmy Carter.

Q: Only seven players have pitched perfect games since 1970. Name the players, the teams they played for, and the year the game occurred.

Q: What was the first professional team to be owned and operated by a woman?

Q: At the start of the 2000 season, what active players belonged to the 3,000-hit club?

Q: True or False: Walter Johnson holds the record for the most consecutive scoreless innings pitched at fifty-six innings.

Q: When questioned about whether he used a foreign substance on the ball, what longtime Dodger pitcher replied, "Vaseline is made right here in the U.S."?

A: Player:

Player:	Played For:	Year:
Len Barker	Cleveland Indians	1981
Mike Witt	California Angels	1984
Tom Browning	Cincinnati Reds	1988
Dennis Martinez	Montreal Expos	1991
Kenny Rogers	Texas Rangers	1994
David Wells	New York Yankees	1998
David Cone	New York Yankees	1999

A: The Newark Eagles of the Negro League. Effa Manley, along with her husband, Abe, ran the well-known team from 1936 to 1948.

A: Wade Boggs and Tony Gwynn—who both made the grade in 1999.

A: False. Orel Hershiser pitched 59 scoreless innings for Los Angeles in 1988.

A: Don Sutton.

Q: Can you match these quotes from professional baseball players?
1. "I don't want to be one of those great players who
   never made the Series."
2. "If I played there, they'd name a candy bar after me."
3. "He (Frank Robinson as a manager) can step on
   your shoes, but he doesn't mess up your shine."
4. "A full mind is an empty bat."
5. "Pitchers like poets, are born not made."
PLAYERS:
a. Reggie Jackson (on his desire to play in New York).
b. Ty Cobb   d. Rickey Henderson
c. Branch Rickey   e. Joe Morgan

Q: Can you name the first five players inducted into the
Hall of Fame? Give the teams they went in under for
extra credit.

Q: At twenty-five and eleven, the New York Yankees
hold the record for the most World Series won (and
lost) by a franchise. Who holds the number two slot?

A: 1-d, 2-a, 3-e, 4-c, 5-b

A: Walter Johnson (Washington Senators)
   Ty Cobb (Detroit Tigers)
   Christy Mathewson (NY Giants)
   Babe Ruth (NY Yankees)
   Honus Wagner (Pittsburgh Pirates)

A: Philadelphia/Kansas City/Oakland A's are at nine wins
   and five losses, and the St. Louis Cardinals are at nine and
   six.

Q: True or False: They're a big business today, but baseball cards originally began as advertising inserts in
cigarettes.

Q: True or False: The most valuable baseball card in the
world is one of Honus Wagner.

Q: Name the only player in baseball history to win batting championships his first two years in the majors.

Q: Who holds the record for the most consecutive
Gold Gloves for an outfielder?

Q: Which of the following terms is NOT a name for a
weakly hit fly ball that just makes it over the infield?
    a. Bloop
    b. Blooper
    c. Bleeder
    d. Dying Quail
    e. Texas Leaguer

A: True.

A: True. The 1909 T206 Honus Wagner baseball card in mint condition has sold for over one million dollars.

A: Tony Oliva of the Minnesota Twins, who hit .323 in 1964 and .321 in 1965.

A: Roberto Clemente (Pittsburgh) and Willie Mays (New York, San Francisco) tie for this honor. They won twelve each.

A: c.

Q: Baseball is foremost a game of rules. Answer true or false to the statements below.

    a. If the pitcher drops the ball, it is always ruled a balk.

    b. A pitcher must deliver the ball within twenty seconds of receiving it from the umpire or catcher when the bases are empty.

    c. The infield-fly rule can only be called by the umpire when there are less than two outs, base runners on first and second (and sometimes third), and the ball is hit in the air to an infielder.

    d. The game can only commence when the umpire yells "Play ball!"

Q: Which infield position typically calls for the smallest glove?

Q: How did Shoeless Joe Jackson get his nickname?

Q: What wizardly shortstop holds the major-league record for lifetime infield assists with 8,375, in addition to the National League record for most Gold Gloves (13)?

A: a. False. It is only a balk if the pitcher drops the ball with a man on base while attempting to deliver a pitch.

b. True.

c. False. The ball must only be deemed as fair and easily caught for the infield-fly rule to apply.

d. False. The umpire need only say "Play" to commence the game—once he sees all defensive players in position and the first batter in the box.

A: Second base—where a smaller glove allows for quicker release of the ball for double plays, for example.

A: He took off his shoes in a minor-league game because they were causing him blisters. No one noticed until he slid into third with a triple, and a fan of the opposing team yelled, "You shoeless son of a gun!"

A: Ozzie Smith.

Q: Which of the following term(s) do NOT refer to strikeouts?
- a. Punchout
- b. K
- c. Whiff
- d. Sayonara
- e. Sit-down pitch

Q: What three players have won the MVP Award at two different positions?

Q: Name the hitters who slugged fifty or more home runs in a season—two or more times in the 1990s.

Q: Who hit the first indoor home run in Houston's Astrodome?

Q: For extra credit, who hit the first home run in the Astrodome's replacement, Enron Field?

A: d and e.

A: Detroit's Hank Greenberg at first base (1935) and in left field (1940); Stan Musial of the St. Louis Cardinals in the outfield (1943, 1948) and at first base (1946); and Milwaukee's Robin Yount at shortstop (1982) and as out-fielder/designated hitter (1989).

A: Mark McGwire in 1996, 1997, 1998, 1999; Sammy Sosa in 1998 and 1999; and Ken Griffey Jr. in 1997 and 1998.

A: New York Yankee Mickey Mantle hit the Astrodome's first homer April 9, 1965, during an exhibition game against the Houston Astros. Despite his homer, the Astros won. The first home run in an official game in the "Dome" was hit by Philadelphia's Richie Allen three days later.

A: In an exhibition game on March 30, 2000, the Astros beat the Yankees again for the first game at Enron Field, with the Astros' Daryle Ward getting the first homer in the eighth inning. As for the first official homer, Scott Rolen hit one for the Phillies in the top of the sixth to lead Philadelphia to a 4–1 victory in the first game at Enron Field on April 7.

Q: Name the nine pitchers voted into the All-Century Dream Team.

Q: True or False: Of all of the current major-league stadiums, Yankee Stadium boasts the greatest seating capacity at 57,545.

Q: Name the two expansion teams who entered the American League in 1977.

Q: Can you match these musings on baseball with their literary speakers?
1. "Baseball is a game played by idiots for morons."
2. "They can't yank a novelist like they can a pitcher. A novelist has to go the full nine, even if it kills him."
3. "The whole history of baseball has the quality of mythology."
4. "Baseball made me understand what patriotism was about, at its best."
CHOICES:
a. Philip Roth   c. Bernard Malamud
b. F. Scott Fitzgerald   d. Ernest Hemingway

A: Nolan Ryan
      Sandy Koufax
      Cy Young
      Roger Clemens
      Bob Gibson
      Walter Johnson
      Warren Spahn
      Christy Mathewson
      Lefty Grove

A: False. The Phillies's Veterans Stadium boasts the greatest seating capacity at 62,382.

A: Toronto Blue Jays and Seattle Mariners.

A: 1-b, 2-d, 3-c, 4-a